HERBS: HOW TO GROW, TREAT AND USE THEM

OVEN TEMPERATURES

F	C	GAS	TYPE
150°	70°	Lowest	cold
175°	80°	Lowest	cold
200°	100°	Lowest +	cold +
225°	110°	¼	very cool
250°	130°	½	
275°	140°	1	cool
300°	150°	2	
325°	170°	3	very moderate
350°	180°	4	moderate
375°	190°	5	moderate to
400°	200°	6	moderately hot
425°	220°	7	hot
450°	230°	8	
475°	240°	9	very hot
500°	250°	–	
525°	250°	–	
550°	290°	–	

METRIC CONVERSION

WEIGHT		VOLUME	
1 Ounce	25 grams		
2 Ounce	50 grams	⅛ Pint	60 Millilitre
3 Ounce	75 grams	¼ Pint	125 Millilitre
4 Ounce	100 grams	½ Pint	250 Millilitre
5 Ounce	125 grams	¾ Pint	375 Millilitre
6 Ounce	150 grams	1 Pint	500 Millilitre
7 Ounce	175 grams		
8 Ounce	200 grams		

½ Pound—200-250 grams.

1 Pound—500 grams.

1 ounce—25 grams as advised by The Metrication Working Party of the United Kingdom Federation for Education in Home Economics.

HERBS: HOW TO GROW, TREAT AND USE THEM

by

ETHELIND FEARON

BARRIE & JENKINS
COMMUNICA-EUROPA

by Barrie & Jenkins Ltd

This edition published in 1977
by Barrie & Jenkins Ltd
24 Highbury Crescent
London N5 1RX

ISBN 0 214 20309 3

Printed by Thomson Litho Ltd, East Kilbride,
Scotland

CONTENTS

"Cooking means the knowledge of all fruits and herbs and balms and spices; it means carefulness and inventiveness, and watchfulness and willingness and readiness of appliance. It means the economy of your grandmothers and the science of the modern chemists—it means much tasting and no wasting."

JOHN RUSKIN

CHAPTER ONE

HISTORICAL

" *Anything green which grew out of the mould*
Was an excellent herb to our fathers of old."

KIPLING

IT all depends on what you *call* a herb. I have seen recipes in some quite famous herbals which depended for their sole herbal ingredient on such various items as orange peel; onions; rose and violet petals; mulberries; pine branches; cucumber; verbena; tomato and broom sprigs.

Actually any *herbage* is logically and demonstrably a *herb*, and it therefore follows that anything which grows is liable to inclusion in a herb book. But one must draw a line somewhere, and I propose to draw it firmly at the door of any ordinary kitchen. All culinary enticements of a vegetable nature which can be grown in an average garden and used in an average household to enliven the average dullness of the all-too-average meal may, can, and doubtless will, be included. And all outlandish herbage such as tropical leaves, seeds, and roots; all herbal-medical remedies, love philtres, magicks, ancient syrups, essences, cosmetics, cordials, elegant poisons, sweetmeats and suchlike interesting antiquities, will be perforce rejected (temporarily) with the hope of dabbling in the subject at some later date.

Which leaves us with a clear case for angelica, aniseed, balm, basil, bay, bergamot, borage, carraway, chervil, chives, coriander, corn salad, costmary, cumin, dill, elecampane, fennel, garlic, juniper, lavender, lemon-verbena, marigold, marjoram, mint of various kinds, nasturtium, peppermint, pimento, pimpernel, penny royal, purslane, rampion, rocket, rosemary, rue, saffron, sage, salad-burnet, savory, sorrel, tarragon, thyme and watercress.

And enough to be going on with, too. Though the ancients had a much more interesting repertoire and the sixteenth and seventeenth century housewife was required not only to dry and distil a terrifying selection of herbs for food but to render them into medicines for everything from broken legs and bad temper to snake bite and surfeit, and into pomades, perfumes, pills and pot-pourris. So that the house was competely provisioned against all eventualities by its own herb garden, which *was* the garden, and no nonsense about growing flowers to look at if they hadn't some more practical use as well.

The medieval reaction to any plant was the same as the first question one asks in the game of Twenty Questions: " Can you eat it? " And meals were all the more interesting—not to say adventurous—on that account. In a day when the word " herbs " means to most of us a dry and dusty and anonymous mixture out of a packet, a bit more medievalism wouldn't do any harm, and I will try to steer a fair course between the ancient and the modern, although in order to curtail the flood of ordinary and everyday recipes and keep the booklet within reasonable dimensions I must exclude the obvious. We will assume, if you please, that you already serve parsley with cod, mint with lamb, horseradish with beef and capers with mutton. Only those recipes which include some other herb or combination of herbs, *as well as* the foregoing—or else use a single herb in some original way—will be allowed to creep in. And for the same reason I will assume that you can cook, and we will keep the instructions and directions as snappy as possible. That way we get more variety into less space and it is more interesting for all of us. But before you can cook a thing you must first grow it, so perhaps an alphabetical aid to herb gardening should now follow.

CHAPTER TWO

BOTANICAL

"*The Sun was lord of the Marigold,*
Basil and Rocket belonged to Mars."

KIPLING

". . . it is under the dominion of Saturn and is an excellent qualifyer of the unruly actions and passions of Venus, though Mars should also join with her. And by the icon or image of every herb the ancients at first found out their virtues. Modern writers laugh at them for it, but I wonder how the virtues of herbs came at first to be known if not by their signatures; the moderns have them from the writings of the ancients; the ancients had no writings to have them from."—CULPEPER.

IT is quite easy to see the connection between the sun and most pot-herbs. Their most distinctive quality is an essential oil which develops in exact proportion to the sunlight they receive, and for this reason a very flourishing herb garden can easily be created on some dry and meagre plot unsuitable for any more luscious vegetation. Not only *can* be, in fact *must* be, for herbs grown on dark rich soil or in a shaded situation are quite unrecognizable as the stocky pungently-scented plants which perfume the sunbaked stony screes of the Mediterranean.

Prepare the herb garden, then, in poor, hot soil, if possible facing south. Let there be a windbreak on north and east, to shelter from wind and frost, and open ground to west and south to admit the sun, and if you can contrive to have ground *sloping* to the south there can be no better situation, because the heat-lovers can wallow in open sun on the upper section, and below them, where rainfall will naturally drain and shade shelter their roots, can lurk the mint and lettuces, sorrel, angelica, chervil, watercress, horseradish, celery, bergamot and balm. Make yourself a little plan for planting and you can't go wrong.

If you happen to know the country of origin of each of these plants (a piece of research which would comfortably occupy the winter evenings and lead you a fascinating geographical-historical dance) you can reproduce to their liking their original growing conditions. But failing time for this the leaf is a rough guide. You will find, with few exceptions, that the hard-wooded twiggy plant with small aromatic leaves is a sun-lover, whose volatile oils will not properly develop unless it is baked and starved (for instance, rosemary and thyme), and the soft-stemmed large or lush-leaved herb loves shade and moisture, like angelica and spearmint.

Nasturtium, a native of Peru, is an exception and a sun-lover, but we will run through them briefly and alphabetically and say of each which piece to use and in what state.

Angelica. Russian. Damp and shady spot. Young stems are peeled and candied, or added, chopped-up, to rhubarb jam. Essential oil from the seed is used in liqueurs, but that need not bother us. At least, not here.

Aniseed. Slightly delicate. Sow in spring on warm border. The seed is gathered in August, dried, and scattered over pancakes, salads, soups and young carrots, also on the tops of cakes.

Balm. Greek. Grows anywhere. Branches are hung up to dry and leaves powdered for fish sauces, stuffings or as a substitute for lemons. Leaves are used green in salads and summer drinks.

Basil. Indian. Is tender and has a scent and savour delicately clove-like. Seeds, sown in heat, are planted out at the same time as tomatoes. Can be used sparingly green in salads or chopped to sprinkle over fish, or dried for stuffings, etc.

Bay. Italian. Will grow as a bush or tree anywhere from cuttings. One of the essential ingredients of a " bouquet garni " and of milk puddings, one or two leaves used whole, and removed before serving.

Bergamot. American. Grown like mint. Likes sun and also a deep rich soil. An odd leaf or two enlivens a salad or a summer drink, and the dried leaves make a delicious tisane.

Borage. Native plant liking poor, stony soil. Both this and Bergamot are notably excellent for bees as well as for claret-cup. Use flowers and leaves.

Carraway. North European. Grows anywhere from seeds as a biennial. Dry seeds and use in cakes, bread and mixed with cream cheeses.

Chervil. My favourite salad herb, tasting of aniseed and growing from seed anywhere. Use small successional sowings and water frequently in dry weather. Origin unknown. Used green for salads, soups and sauces, and dried, like parsley, for stuffings.

Chives. Alpine. Pretty little edging plant, growing anywhere from bulbs or divided plants. Used green for its mild oniony flavour and unrepetitive qualities. Excellent for salads.

Coriander. Indian. Grows in light rich soil from spring-sown seed. Seeds are an ingredient of curry and delicious sprinkled on cakes and bread, milk puddings and cream cheeses. Tastes rather like dried orange peel. Leaves are used in soups and salads, and must be gathered young; therefore monthly sowings are advisable.

Corn-salad, otherwise known as "Lambs' lettuce". Native. Will (and does) grow almost anywhere, for instance, on corn stubbles in autumn. Sow in September for use during winter with beetroot in a salad. But do not obscure its delicate flavour by herding it into a bowl with parsley, chervil and rocket. Just stick to beetroot.

Costmary. Middle European. Will grow anywhere from stolons, like mint. Leaves used dried in stuffings, particularly veal, and fresh in sauces and soups. Useful ingredient of pot-pourri.

Cumin. Egypt. Rather similar in flavour and its umbelliferous habit to carraway and coriander. Sow seed in sunny place monthly. Grows quickly Use the dry seeds for pickles and spices.

Dill. Hardy annual of Mediterranean origin. Used in pickles and as a substitute for carraway seed. Its young leaves may be employed (with caution) to give a carraway flavour to sauces (especially with fish) and soups.

Elecampane. Himalayan. Grows everywhere. Plant roots in autumn and increase by division. The roots taste faintly of violet and are candied.

Fennel. Native. Sow in sunny spot. Use tender leaves for fish and sauces. Seeds are also used for flavouring and the thick, fleshy leaf-stalks either cooked like celery or shredded in salad.

Garlic. Siberia. Can be grown in England like onions, but is then coarse and rather strong. The most delicious is Mediterranean, and it is quite indispensable to many of the finest sauces and salads. But use it with discretion.

Good King Henry (whose proper name is Chenopodium) is not much known except on the east coast of England. It is a native perennial and enjoys rich cool soil. If earthed up in early spring the blanched shoots are eaten like asparagus. Later the young leaves are cooked like spinach or used raw in salads. Like asparagus, if the shoots are at all tough their bottoms must be scraped before cooking.

Juniper. Being a native plant, grows anywhere. The beautiful blue-green frond-like foliage bears berries which remain green for two years and are only fit for use when they turn blue-black in their second autumn. They are used in cooking game (venison, hare, pheasant and woodcock, because all these in life enjoy eating juniper berries if they can come by them), and are crushed into the pan as an aromatic ingredient of the gravy.

Lavender. European. Needs sun and poor soil. Grows from September cuttings or seed. Used mainly in pot-pourri, but also as candied flowers for cake decorations.

Lemon-verbena. Southern Europe. Best grown against a wall. The deliciously lemon-scented young leaves in fruit drinks, jellies and salads are very refreshing in summer, and can be cooked with lemon-rind in sauces for fish or veal.

Marigold. Indian. Sow seed in spring. Likes poor sunny soil. Fresh petals and chopped young leaves give a delightful tang to salads, and the dried petals in a bread-pudding make it really worth eating.

Marjoram. Mediterranean. Dry, hot position. Sow seed in spring or divide perennial plants. One of the " bouquet garni " herbs and used dried in most stuffings.

Mint or, more properly, Spearmint. Likes damp and shade. Grows easily from stolons. Used fresh for sauces and to cook with young peas and potatoes or serve with iced drinks. Also dried for winter use.

Apple mint and *pineapple mint* are variations of the above, with leaves round instead of pointed and more hairy. Has a much more delicate and fruity flavour. Make a new mint bed every year or it will die away.

Nasturtium. Peru. Likes hot, poor soil. Young leaves and flowers delicious in salads, and the seeds, pickled when young and green, are a perfect substitute for capers.

Parsley. Greek. Likes a damp, shady position. Grows easily from seed sown yearly. Used fresh in salads, sauces and stuffings and dried for winter use; but dry it *quickly* to preserve the green colour, and do use the tender, uncurled French kind, *not* the fuzzy garnishing sort, which has the resilience and endurance of a pan-scrubber.

Peppermint. Indigenous. Likes a rich, damp soil. Used dried for flavouring sweets, etc. Store the dried leaves in jars.

Pimento. Spanish. Treat like tomatoes and use cooked.

Pimpernel. Wild, but will grow anywhere in a garden. The small, fleshy leaves are delicious in salads.

Pennyroyal. Native perennial. A delicious little creeping peppermint. Damp and shady spot. Use the tender tips of shoots in salads—sparingly.

Purslane. Mediterranean. Sunny situation and poor soil. Sow seed in spring and use the young leaves in salad. When cut down it will shoot out again.

Rampion. Native. Treat like lettuce but do not sow too early. June 1st is soon enough in a rich light soil. Use leaves and roots in winter salads. The leaves are very much like the common corn-salad and the flavour of the crisp roots is hot like radishes.

Rocket. European. Fairly moist soil and tastes better if watered when weather is dry. Sow in succession from April to September and use tender leaves and young tips in salad. Delicious, but apparently unknown as a salad ingredient in England.

Romaine. The large black-seeded cos lettuce. Used green in salads and also boiled.

Rosemary. Mediterranean. Can be grown in a dry sunny spot, either from seed or cuttings and used as ornamental shrub. The dried leaves are a useful ingredient of veal stuffings and the " bouquet garni," but do not overdo it.

Rue. Mediterranean. Sunny, dry situation. Grow from cuttings and use *very* sparingly in salad. The dried leaves used *sparsely* between bread and butter make an unusual sandwich.

Saffron. British. The dried pistils of the crocus-like flowers flavour and colour cakes, but so many are required to have any effect that it is grown more for ornament than use. If you want to *use* saffron get it from a chemist.

Sage. Mediterranean. Hot, dry spot. Roots easily from cuttings. Used dried in stuffings for pork and duck and sparingly as fresh leaves chopped on to porridge or in a sandwich.

Salad Burnet. Originally South European but now universal. Grows wild. Sun and starvation-lover. Leaves used fresh, chopped into a salad. Flowers used for home-made wine. Fragrant when trodden underfoot. Leaves impart a delicious cucumber flavour to hock cup.

Sorrel. French. Likes heavy soil and partial shade. Delicious lemon-flavoured young leaves in salad or boiled like spinach or made into soup. Sow seed in spring and manure well.

Savory. Mediterranean. The summer savory is an annual and the winter is evergreen and perennial. Delicious aromatic herb to dry and use in stuffings, etc., or use fresh with fish, cheese and eggs. Does best on poor soil.

Tarragon. French perennial, originally Siberian. Likes dry, sunny spot. Grow from cuttings. Leaves may be used fresh in a "bouquet garni " or dried for winter use.

Thyme. Mediterranean perennial. Hot, dry

soil. Grow from cuttings or division, and use in stuffings for veal, poultry and fish, and dried for a winter pot-herb.

Watercress. Native. Usually grows in running water but will do very well in a deeply-dug moist trench with plenty of humus (leaf-mould, spent hops or compost). Grows from cuttings. Used in salad, sandwiches and soups.

HERBS—HOW TO TREAT THEM

To dry herbs they should be cut when the essential oils are at their state of greatest abundance and perfection and the whole plant bursting with health and well-being. This is obviously just at flowering point, since, once this is accomplished, all plants go downhill towards death, their purpose fulfilled. Catch them, then, with their flowers just expanding on a dry, warm morning, and dry them quickly to preserve flavour, but *never* by the heat of a stove.

Tie in small bunches so that the air can reach every part and hang in a current of air but out of the sun.

A very good place is on a rod or line suspended below the roof of an outside shed in an air current but out of cold draughts. Inspect periodically in case the leaves have caught some dampness and are turning mouldy, and if they are exposed to dew bring them indoors before nightfall.

About ten days' hanging should be sufficient to dry them (since over-drying ruins the flavour), after which they are crumbled between the hands over clean white paper so that you can remove all twiggy bits, weeds or insects, and stored in airtight bottles (old salad cream or hair-cream bottles are excellent). Any moisture forming on the inside of the bottle is a signal that herbs are not properly dry, and they should be tipped out on to clean white paper and given a further drying spell. It is also well to *label* the bottles, however certain you are that you can remember which is which. They will keep their flavour, if necessary, for years.

If you have no shed, a concrete path in full sun will do as well. Spread a layer of newspaper on the path, scatter the freshly-gathered herbs on the paper, spread old lace curtain netting over them, weighted all round with bricks or dictionaries, and set an electric fan to blow on them. By the combination of bottom warmth and top draught they should be dry enough to crumble in four hours, and may be immediately stored in jars. Their flavour is at its very best with this quick drying.

Perhaps your garden space is very restricted, in which case it is best to restrict proportionately the number of herbs. A space ten feet by two feet will grow a sufficiency of parsley, mint, chives, marjoram, thyme, rocket, summer savory, one sage bush, a plant of pennyroyal, and a patch of chervil. If no garden at all, you can still grow parsley, mint, chives, pennyroyal and chervil in a window-box, with a sage bush at one end and thyme at the other.

Do not try to dry fennel, chervil or coriander shoots, dry and use the seeds instead; and this applies to parsley, too, if it is the English curled. But the French kind dries well.

CHAPTER THREE

ANALYTICAL

Balm : the leaves drunk with wine are good against the stingings of venemous beasts and the biting of mad dogs, and are likewise good for those that cannot take breath unless they hold their necks upright.

DIOSCORIDES

Baume maketh the heart merry and joy full and strengtheneth the vitall spiritts, it is singular good for the heart and the infirmities thereof.

AVICEN

Chervil : the leaves are exceeding good, wholesome and pleasant among other sallad herbs, giving the taste of Anise seed to the rest. The roots are likewise most excellent in a sallad if they be boiled and dressed as the cunning Cooke knoweth how better than myselfe, notwithstanding I use to eat them with oils and vinegar being first boiled, which is very good for old people that are dull and without courage: it rejoiceth and comforteth the heart and increaseth their lust and strength.

GERARD

Dill stayeth the hiccup being boiled in wine and but smelled unto, being tied in a cloth.

CULPEPER

Elecampane is good for them that are bursten and troubled with cramps and convulsions.

GERARD

Endive is available for the faintings, swoonings and passions of the heart. It cannot be used amiss. CULPEPER

Fennel. Both leaves, seeds, and roots thereof are much used in drink or broth to make people more lean that are too fat. Wild fennel is stronger and hotter than the tame.

CULPEPER

Horse-radish. The root bruised and laid to the place grieved with the sciatica, joint ach, or the hard swellings of the liver and spleen, doth wonderfully help them all. CULPEPER

Lavender the chemical oil is of so fierce and piercing a quality that some few drops are sufficient to be given with other things either for inward or outward griefs. GERARD

Lettuce taken before meat it doth many times stir up appetite, and eaten after supper it keepeth away drunkennesse which cometh by wine.

MARTIAL

Marjoram the leaves boiled in water and the decoction drunk easeth such as are given to overmuch singing. GERARD

Mint. The smell of mint doth stir up the mind and the taste to a greedy desire of meat. Mint is marvellous wholesome for the stomach. It is good against watering eyes if poured into the ears with honeyed water. PLINY

Nasturtium is of so great beauty and sweetnesse withall that my Garden of delight cannot bee unfurnished of it. The Spaniards and others use the leaves thereof in stead of ordinary Cresses, because the taste is somewhat sharpe, agreeing thereunto.

PARKINSON

Rocket is for the most part eaten with Lettuce Purslane or such cold herbs and not alone because of its heat and strength. The seed bruised and mixed with a little vinegar and the gall of an Oxe, cleanseth the face of freckles, spots and blew marks, that come by beatings, fals, or otherwaies.

PARKINSON

Romane red Lettice is the best and greatest of them all. John Tradescante that first brought it to England did write untoe me that after one of them had been bound and whited, when the refuse was cut away, the rest weighed seventeen ounces. But it *must* be whited that it eat kindly.

PARKINSON

Saffron is an herbe of the Sun and under the Lion, therefore you need not demand a reason why it strengthens the heart so exceedingly.

CULPEPER

Sage is of excellent use to help the memory, warming and quickening the senses, and the Conserve made of the flowers is used to the same purpose. It causeth the hair to become black.

CULPEPER

Savory. Mercury claims the dominion over this herb and there is no better remedy against the colic . . . it quickens dull spirits in a lethargy . . . and also taketh away the pain that comes by stinging of bees etc.

CULPEPER

Sorrel is prevalent in all hot diseases and to refresh the spirits overspent with the violence of furious or fiery fits of agues, to quench thirst and to procure an appetite in fainting or decayed stomachs, for it resisteth the putrefaction of the blood, killeth worms and is a cordiall to the heart.

CULPEPER

Tansy fried with eggs as is the custom in Spring helpeth to digest and carry downward the bad humours that trouble the stomach. Being boiled in oil it is good for the sinews shrunk by cramp or pained with cold.

CULPEPER

Tarragon is altogether used among other cold herbes, to temper their coldnesse, and they to temper its heat, so to give the better rellish untoe the Sallet. There are some Authors that have held Tarragon not to be an herbe of its owne kinde, but that it was first produced by putting the seede of Lin or Flaxe into the roote of an Onion.

PARKINSON

Thyme is excellent good for those that are troubled with the gout. It easeth pains in the loins and hips.

CULPEPER

The Vine. The leaves of the English vine being boiled, make a good lotion for sore mouths; being boiled with barley meal into a poultice it cools inflammation of wounds; the dropping of the vine when it is cut in the spring, which country people call tears, being boiled in syrup with sugar and taken inwardly, is excellent to stay pregnant women's longings after every thing they see. The decoction of vine leaves in white wine doth the like; also the tears of the vine drunk two or three spoonfuls at a time, breaks the stone in the bladder. This is a very good remedy and it is well done to kill a vine to cure a man, but the salt of the leaves is held to be better. The ashes of the burnt branches will make teeth that are as black as a coal to be as white as snow if you but every morning rub them with it. It is a gallant tree of the sun, very sympathetic with the body of man.

CULPEPER

Water cress pottage is a good remedy to cleanse the blood in the spring and helps headaches and consumes the gross humours winter hath left behind. If any fancy not pottage they may eat the herb as a salad.

CULPEPER

CHAPTER FOUR

PRACTICAL

THERE is no section of a meal, from hors d'œuvres to junket or savoury, which cannot be improved by the intelligent addition of herbs, and this is particularly noticeable among soups, but " discretion " is the operative principle here; good herbs are so strong and full of flavour that a quarter or half teaspoonful usually suffices. For instance, in **Basil Soup**, one sprig is sufficient to give its distinctive flavour to the whole brew.

2 pints water
1 turnip
1 branch celery
1 clove garlic
Seasoning
1 b. potatoes
½ lb. young French beans
1 lb. tomatoes
1 sprig sweet basil
Vermicelli

Cut all the vegetables finely, remove tomato seeds, add salt and pepper, and simmer all for ½ hour. Chop garlic and basil, mix with a little olive oil to a smooth paste and add to soup, with the vermicelli broken small. Cook another 15 minutes and serve with grated cheese.

Barley Broth (Armenian)

2 quarts bone stock
2 large onions
1 cup pearl barley
2 medium leeks
1 teaspoonful mint
½ lb. carrots
2 teaspoonfuls parsley
2 oz. bone marrow or butter

Chop all finely. Add salt and pepper to taste and cook slowly until barley is soft.

Bean Soup (Italian)

2 pints water
½ lb. skinned broad beans
1 onion
1 bay leaf
2 cloves crushed garlic
1 lb. fresh haricot beans
1 lb. tomatoes
¼ lb. fat bacon
1 sprig of thyme
2 teaspoonfuls parsley

Shell beans and skin broad beans; mince bacon, garlic, parsley, and tie thyme and bay leaf together so that they can be removed easily; chop tomatoes and onion and after frying in oil add to the other ingredients in the water. Season well and simmer half an hour. Just before serving, strain soup, mash vegetables, put all together again and pour over some fried croutons of bread which are waiting in a hot tureen.

Bonne Femme Soup (French)

Peel, slice and salt a small cucumber, then drain off its moisture and put in a casserole with a shredded lettuce, a branch each of tarragon and chervil and two leaves of lemon verbena. Put lid on casserole and cook gently without water until cucumber is soft. Add two pints of chicken broth or any white stock and thicken with cornflour. Leave in a hot place to thicken without boiling and stir to keep the texture smooth. Finally add ½ pint milk and ¼ pint cream, testing for seasoning. Leave a few moments longer to reheat, but never let it boil as this makes the cucumber bitter.

Brodetto (Italian)

2 pints mutton broth
2 teaspoonfuls lemon juice
¼ teaspoonful fresh marjoram
4 egg yolks
4 teaspoonfuls grated Parmesan cheese
1 small sprig basil, fennel and tarragon

Beat egg yolks until smooth, Add lemon juice, pepper, and salt, then pour a little of the hot broth over, mixing it in gently to prevent curdling. When all is mixed add chopped herbs and cook very gently five minutes to thicken, stirring constantly. Scatter toast squares in each hot soup plate, pour brodetto over and scatter cheese on top of each before serving.

Carraway Soup (Hungarian)

2 pints water
2 lb. diced potatoes
¼ pint sour cream
2 tablespoonfuls flour
½ pint sour milk
¼ teaspoonful carraway seeds

Boil seeds in water. Add milk and slaked flour and cook until thickened. Add sour cream and potatoes which have been boiled separately. Season and serve.

Celery Cream Soup

1 head of celery — *1 medium onion*
2 pints white stock or water — *1 oz. flour*
½ pint milk — *Bouquet garni*
Chopped parsley — *1 oz. fat*

Slice celery and onion and cook until soft in fat without browning. Add stock and bouquet garni, which is a sprig each of thyme, marjoram, and parsley and a bay leaf (with a blade of mace) tied in a little bit of muslin for easy removal, and simmer gently until vegetables are tender. Sieve and return to saucepan, with flour slaked in the milk and seasoning to taste. Cook gently 5 minutes. Scatter the freshly chopped parsley on the surface of each plate before serving.

Chick Pea Soup (American)

2 pints water or stock
2 tablespoonfuls olive oil
1 clove chopped garlic
4 anchovy fillets chopped
1 lb. dried peas soaked overnight
2 tablespoonfuls tomato paste
½ teaspoonful chopped rosemary
2 tablespoonfuls cheese grated.

Cook peas in water until tender, or use a

can of haricot beans if preferred. Sieve. Brown the garlic, rosemary, anchovies in the oil and add the tomato paste. Add all to peas or beans and season well. Serve with cheese.

Chiffonade (French)

2 pints stock
1 lettuce
1 handful spinach
2 oz. butter
1 handful sorrel
1 teaspoonful chopped chervil

Cook chopped lettuce in the butter with only the water in which it was washed. Add the chopped sorrel and spinach which together should be roughly the same quantity as the lettuce. Cook with the lettuce about five minutes then add all to the hot stock. Serve with the chervil floating on top, after checking for seasoning.

Cress Soup (French)

Cook a pound of potatoes. Mash, add a bunch of washed and chopped watercress leaves but no stalks, one medium onion cooked in butter without browning, a shake of nutmeg, two egg yolks blended with lemon juice and cream, seasoning and, very gradually, enough milk to make thin and smooth. Reheat without boiling and sprinkle with chopped chervil before serving.

Fish Soup (French)

2 lb. fish or 2 cods' heads
1 onion, 1 leek, 2 branches celery
Bayleaf, parsley, chervil, garlic, saffron, olive oil, fennel
¼ lb. vermicelli
2 pints water
½ lb. tomatoes

Mince onion and leek, skin and de-seed tomatoes. Tie celery and herbs into a bunch and wash fish or cods' heads. Cook vegetables in the oil until soft then add fish, cooking for five minutes, and lastly herbs, seasoning, crushed garlic (one or two cloves according to how much you like it) and gradually the water. Cook gently for half an hour then sieve into a clean saucepan. If cods' heads, their use is then finished, but if a lump of fish you may like to salvage the bits and include them with the soup, even though their nourishment is gone into the liquid. Bring soup to the boil, throw in the vermicelli and cook gently until it is soft. Test again for seasoning and serve very hot with a sprinkle of chopped parsley on top.

Goulash Soup (Hungarian)

1 lb. shin of beef
2 oz. fat for frying
2 large onions
1 tablespoonful vinegar
3 pints water
2 tablespoonfuls flour
½ lb. potatoes

¼ teaspoonful paprika
Marjoram, carraway seeds and seasoning

Slice onions and fry in the fat. Cut meat into cubes and add to pan, with vinegar, paprika, chopped herbs and enough water to cover. Put lid on pan and cook gently until beef is tender. Peel and cube the potatoes, stir in flour and when blended add rest of water and test for flavour, adding more salt if necessary. Add potatoes and cook a few minutes until soft but not smashed

If you prefer this dish pinker double the quantity of paprika and use also a tablespoonful of tomato *purée*.

Hot Broth (Hungarian)

2 pints stock
½ lb. skinned and de-seeded tomatoes or one can, sieved
6 peppercorns
½ lb. onions
3 cloves
Cinnamon, garlic, bayleaf, marjoram, tarragon, rosemary.

Cook the onion gently in butter in an iron pan. Add the tomato, chopped herbs, cloves and peppercorns, crushed garlic to taste, salt and ½ teaspoonful paprika, putting in the bayleaf whole with cotton tied to it so that it can be removed. Add the stock and cook gently half an hour. Strain and add a handful of pearl barley. Cook again until this is soft, check for flavour and serve with a sprinkle of fresh parsley on top.

Potage Julienne (French)

2 pints water or stock
1 turnip
2 small onions
½ head of celery
1 handful lettuce leaves
1 tablespoonful chervil
2 leaves basil
1 large carrot or 2 small ones
2 small leeks
½ cabbage
1 handful sorrel
1 cupful shelled peas
1 teaspoonful parsley
2 oz. butter

Cut in match-strips the carrot, turnip, celery, leeks, and onion, and cook slowly in an iron saucepan with a teaspoonful of castor sugar. When soft, after about half-hour, add half a pint of the stock or water, just enough to cover the contents of pan, and cook another half-hour. Cook cabbage separately for five minutes to remove the strong flavour then shred and add to the rest, pour into pan the remaining stock or water and cook again for ten minutes, Cook the peas separately with the chervil and add, then just before serving, shred the sorrel and lettuce, cook them in the rest of the butter for a few minutes and add to the pot. Check for seasoning and serve with croutons. Vegetables should be fresh and young.

Minestrone (Italian)

1 tablespoonful olive oil
1 chopped clove of garlic
1 teaspoonful chopped parsley
1 teaspoonful chopped rosemary
1 tablespoonful tomato paste
2 sliced carrots
½ lb. haricot beans, cooked
1 large cup shelled peas
¼ lb. chopped salt pork
1 small onion, chopped
1 teaspoonful chopped sage
1 teaspoonful chopped tarragon
4 branches celery, chopped
2 diced potatoes
2 tiny marrows, diced
¼ lb. macaroni

Pour the oil in an iron saucepan, add the pork and cook a few minutes then add all vegetables and herbs and brown slightly in the fat and oil. Add tomato paste thinned down with water, mix well then add 2 pints water or stock and cook slowly until vegetables are soft. Put in broken macaroni and cook ten minutes or until soft. Season highly and serve very hot with a generous sprinkle of cheese on top.

Mozganova (Polish)

Press 1 lb. of calves brain through a coarse sieve. Put 2 oz. of butter in an iron pan, add 2 oz. flour and cook as for sauce, add the sieved brain and a crushed clove of garlic then sufficient white stock or milk to make it thin and smooth. Season well and cook until creamy and flour is swelled, then mix two egg yolks in the tureen with ½ cupful of cream, pour soup on to them and serve with a sprinkle of chopped parsley.

Oyster Soup (Portuguese)

Fish stock
1 egg yolk to each pint
6 oysters to each pint of stock
1 lemon juice
Chopped fennel, tarragon and thyme and a pinch of saffron

Fry the oysters lightly in butter and add them and their liquor to the fish stock together with the chopped herbs and seasoning to taste, including the saffron. Mingle the yolks with a little cream in the soup tureen, add the lemon juice gradually and pour the hot soup over this after it has cooked the oysters gently for about ten minutes. Serve with croutons fried in butter.

Potage St. Germain (French Dried Pea)

2 pints water
1 large leek
1 carrot
¼ lb. streaky bacon
¼ lb. butter
1 lb. split peas soaked over night
1 large onion
1 handful spinach
1 twig of thyme and one bay leaf
1 tablespoonful chopped chervil

Chop bacon and cook in frying pan then add the carrot, onion, the green part of the leek and the spinach, cooking gently in the butter for about ten minutes. Add to the peas and the water in which they were soaked together with the thyme and bayleaf tied together so that they can be removed. Cook gently until the peas are soft, then mash all through a sieve, season, add a handful of fresh green peas which have been cooked separately (frozen ones do quite well), bring to the boil again, add a walnut of butter and the chopped chervil and serve with croutons.

This soup is called **Potage Longchamps** if, instead of fresh peas, one adds a handful of sorrel and two tablespoonfuls of vermicelli, both of which have been cooked separately, just before serving.

Pig's Heart Soup (Italian)

2 lb. pig's heart, diced
1 tablespoonful pork fat from round the kidneys
2 pints water
¼ lb. bacon or ham rind cut up
2 tablespoonfuls tomato paste
½ pint red wine
Rosemary, 1 bay leaf, ½ teaspoonful tarragon

Fry the cut-up heart in an iron pan with the ham rind and pork fat. When well browned add salt and pepper and the wine. Cook until this is absorbed then add the herbs (the bay leaf should be dried and crumbed) and the tomato paste diluted with a little water. Stir for a few moments to mix well then add the water, cover the pan and simmer for 1½ hours. Test for seasoning and pour over croutons in large tureen.

Potage à la Picarde (French)

This is a spring soup of young mixed vegetables.

1 pint water	*1 pint milk*
2 egg yolks	*2 tablespoonfuls cream*
1 lb. potatoes	
1 handful spinach	*1 cos lettuce*
1 handful water cress leaves	*1 handful sorrel*
1 tablespoonful chervil leaves	*6 tarragon leaves*
	4 oz. butter

Wash the lettuce, spinach and sorrel and cook gently with one ounce of the butter. Add the potatoes, diced, then a little water and cook gently until potatoes are soft. Crush with a fork, add the herbs, chopped, the watercress pulled from its stalks leaf by leaf, the rest of the water and milk and enough salt and pepper to season it well. Cook gently ten minutes, stirring occasionally, while you toast some bread, half a slice for each person. Butter it, cut into dice, put into individual soup plates, pour the soup over it and scatter a few chopped watercress leaves over it for a garnish.

Potato Soup (Austrian)

1 lb. potatoes
Bit of bacon or some ham rind
1 tablespoonful chopped parsley
½ teaspoonful chopped tarragon
2 tablespoonfuls flour
2 pints water
1 chopped onion
½ teaspoonful chopped marjoram
2 oz. butter

2 tablespoonfuls sour cream
A grating of nutmeg and a dash of paprika

Peel and dice the potatoes and cook. In an iron pan melt the butter, add the flour and mix well, add the chopped onions and parsley and cook until slightly coloured then add the chopped rind, the potato water, seasoning, herbs and potatoes. Cook all together slowly for an hour. Sieve and add the sour cream. Re-heat but do not allow to boil again. Serve with small dice of crisply fried bread.

Pot-au-Feu (French)

In a heavy iron pan simmer 2 lb. shin or brisket of beef for four hours with a large sliced leek, ½ lb. each of carrot and turnip, one crushed clove of garlic and a large onion in which you stick four cloves. Add enough salt and pepper to flavour well. Strain off the soup with the vegetables cut up in it and in each soup plate have a slice of fried bread over which you pour the hot soup. The meat is reserved for a separate course or left until cold for next day, but if you wish to make the pot-au-feu the main dish, cut a few slices of meat into small dice and put them into the individual plates, too.

Potage Provencal (Southern France)

2 pints water or stock
2 large onions
½ lb. tomatoes
2 oz. vermicelli
Olive oil, garlic, tarragon, bay leaf, small sprig of thyme

In an iron pan put the oil and brown the minced onion and tomato in it. Add the water or stock then the garlic, herbs and seasoning. Boil ½ hour then strain and boil up again. Throw in the vermicelli and poach it quickly in the soup for ten minutes.

Potage Perigourdine (French)
(Pumpkin Soup in English)

2 pints water
1½ lb. haricot beans
1 turnip
2 leeks
¼ lb. streaky bacon
1 clove garlic
½ cup cream
1½ lb. pumpkin
1 small cabbage
2 medium carrots
2 branches celery
1 tablespoonful parsley
Butter for frying
Nutmeg

Soak the beans overnight. Next day put in a saucepan with the water, the vegetables and bacon all chopped together, the crushed garlic, chopped parsley and seasoning, and cook all together gently for two hours. Cut the pumpkin in dice and cook in butter until soft. Add to the soup and cook together for another half-hour. Sieve all ingredients smoothly and re-heat, add a grating of nutmeg and the cream just before serving, but do not allow to boil again.

If, in addition to the cream you finish it with a lump of butter and two egg yolks it is still pumpkin soup but is called **Veloute Bressane.**

Rabbit Bisque (American)

1 small rabbit
1 cup chopped celery
1 red pepper or pimento de-seeded
1 cup cream
Parsley, bay leaf, lemon juice
2 pints water
6 peppercorns
12 oysters and their liquor
½ cup uncooked rice
2 egg yolks

Cut up the rabbit and simmer gently in the water for an hour. Then add the rice, herbs chopped, oysters scalded in their liquor and cut up, celery and pimento chopped and enough salt and pepper to season it. Simmer until the rice is cooked then rub through a sieve, rabbit, oysters, vegetables and everything. Blend the egg-yolks with the cream, add a tablespoonful of lemon juice drop by drop then thin it down with some of the soup, gradually diluting it and finally putting it all into the soup to re-heat but not boil. Undue haste when mixing this egg-lemon-cream dressing with hot soup will be fatal and it will curdle, so take it slowly.

Chicken Peanut Soup (Southern America)

1 boiling fowl
3 tablespoonfuls flour
4 tablespoonfuls butter
1 bouquet garni in a bag
1 cup peanut butter
2 pints water
1 pint milk
4 tablespoonfuls minced celery
1 cup cream
1 tablespoonful parsley
1 minced onion

Stew the bird slowly three hours in the

water with the herbs in a muslin bag. Rub as much as you can of it through a sieve and return to pan. Add flour, slaked with some of the milk, then add rest of milk, onions and celery and cook another 15 minutes, When onions are tender, test soup for seasoning, add cream and the peanut butter and lastly a scatter of fresh parsley on top of tureen.

Shrimp Soup (Italian)

2 pints fish stock made from heads and bones
1 small onion, sliced
3 tablespoonfuls rice
½ cup red wine
1½ lb shrimps
1 small carrot, chopped
¼ lb. butter
Parsley, thyme, bay leaf, tarragon

In half the stock place the shelled shrimps, onion, carrot, chopped herbs (only three leaves of tarragon and ½ teaspoonful of thyme to 1 bay leaf and a tablespoonful of parsley) and cook gently fifteen minutes. Add wine and cook another fifteen minutes. Cook the rice in the other pint of stock, sieve, and return to its stock. Remove from the other saucepan the shrimps (which have been in a muslin bag), pour the stock in which they cooked through a sieve into the rice mixture, return the shrimps to it, add a good dash of cayenne pepper, ¼ teaspoonful of paprika and a small lump of butter, re-heat and serve.

Sorrel Soup (Belgian)

Take a good handful of sorrel, a cos lettuce and a handful of chervil and chop them coarsely then cook in an iron pan in $\frac{1}{4}$ lb. of butter until they are soft. Add gradually two pints of stock, salt and pepper to your taste and let it simmer gently one hour. Rub through a sieve and thicken with a yolk of egg and a bit of butter just before serving. Serve with diced fried bread and a sprinkle of parsley on top of the plates.

Another Sorrel Soup is made with three handfuls of sorrel but no lettuce or chervil. Cook in the same way and thicken with two egg yolks, a little cream and the juice of half a lemon, blended as in the recipe for rabbit bisque.

Tomato Soup

2 pints water
4 rashers streaky bacon or a bit of ham rind
1 onion
$\frac{1}{4}$ teaspoonful powdered thyme
1 teaspoonful chopped parsley
1$\frac{1}{2}$ lbs tomatoes
2 tablespoonfuls flour
$\frac{1}{2}$ bay leaf
1 oz. butter

Roughly cut tomatoes and soften in a pan with the butter. Add herbs and water and cook half an hour. Rub through a sieve, thicken with the flour, first slaking it with cold water, and cook another five minutes, test for seasoning and serve with croutons.

If you use ½ pint of water for the first stage and then when it is sieved and thickened add 1½ pints of milk, thickening with cream at the last, it is cream of tomato. Some people like sugar added but neither the French nor the Italians add sugar to tomatoes.

You can use the prepared tomato *purée* if fresh tomatoes are not obtainable, and the **Viennese** add a cup of red wine.

The following is an **Armenian** version:

Take two pounds of tomatoes quite ripe, cut in half and remove the seeds. Place them in a thick pan with ¼ lb. of butter, a tablespoonful of lemon juice, a bay leaf, a leaf or two of balm and half a teaspoonful of chopped parsley. Over moderate heat, cook and stir the mixture until the tomatoes are a thick, smooth sauce, add a cup of good stock, mix well, and rub all through a sieve. Put back in pan with another pint of stock, seasoning to taste, a grating of nutmeg, a dash of cayenne and a dish of grated cheese served separately.

Tripe Soup (Armenian)

2 quarts water
2 lemons
2 cloves garlic
2 tablespoonfuls parsley
2 lb tripe
2 eggs
2 pints milk
Salt, pepper, paprika

Cook tripe until tender (about three hours gently) in the water with the chopped garlic.

Put tripe through mincer then return to the broth. Beat the eggs in a bowl and add lemon juice little by little (a combination which gives an indescribable flavour) add some broth to it, then some milk, gradually in order to keep the lemony eggs uncurdled, then return all, with salt and pepper to taste, to the pan and heat *very* slowly to almost boiling point, when it should be custard-thick. Pour into individual bowls in each of which you have dropped a gooseberry-sized dab of butter which has had paprika worked into it. Scatter parsley on top of each and they will be a cream groundwork with a topping of pink and green.

Vegetable Soup (Mid-France)

1½ pints water	*1 pint milk*
1 turnip	*3 leeks*
½ lb. potatoes	*½ lb. celeriac*
4 oz. butter	*4 oz. grated cheese*
½ teaspoonful chervil	*3 leaves tarragon*

Cut up all vegetables and put in thick pan with the butter. Have the heat fierce at first to seal them, then put on the lid and cook gently half an hour until they are soft. Add the water and when all is simmered to a soft mass add the milk which should have been previously boiled or it will curdle. Cook another half-hour with the lid off. Toast and butter one slice of bread for each person, cover with grated cheese, brown under the grill and when ready put one slice in each soup plate and pour over it the vegetable soup.

Venison Soup (Armenian)

Make some small meat-balls with 1 lb. minced venison, 2 tablespoonfuls ground rice, 2 tablespoonfuls chopped onion, 1 tablespoonful chopped parsley, 1 teaspoonful chopped tarragon, bound with egg-yolk. They should be about the size of walnuts. Poach them for an hour gently in chicken or mutton broth. Beat two raw eggs, add slowly the juice of two lemons and some of the broth, then gradually the rest of the broth. Make hot again without boiling, pour over the meat-balls and serve.

FISH

Anchois Toulonnaise

is a way they have in the South of France of preparing raw anchovies, which will do at a pinch for sprats. Fillet the anchovies and soak them in good olive oil for three days. Then cut them in crosswise strips and toss them in this dressing: Use the oil in which they soaked and add to it salt and plenty of pepper, French mustard and lemon juice, a tablespoonful of parsley, a teaspoonful of chervil, three leaves of tarragon and a clove of garlic—these herbs being quantities for each four people. They must be all chopped together very finely and then mixed with the oil, the fish being turned over and over in the mixture and left for some hours before serving.

Anchovy Paste

This is a typical Provencal recipe, containing

all their favourite ingredients, which grow so abundantly there. Pound twelve fillets of anchovy soaked in oil as above with twelve pickled in salt, two cloves of garlic, a dozen walnuts, a small onion, six dried figs, a teaspoonful of French mustard, freshly ground, pepper, a teaspoonful of grated lemon rind, a tablespoonful of lemon juice, half a teaspoonful each of thyme, marjoram and tarragon, a teaspoonful of parsley and three juniper berries. All the herbs should be chopped first then pounded in the mortar with the anchovies and finally with three tablespoonfuls of walnut oil if you can get it, otherwise with olive. Add pepper and cayenne to taste but there will probably be salt enough in the pickled anchovies. Spread this delicious mixture thickly on buttered toast. If put in small pots and covered with melted butter it will keep at least a fortnight. Possibly longer, but I find that it is always all eaten long before then anyway.

Bourrida (Italian)

1½ lb. mackerel or any similar fish
4 anchovy fillets, chopped
½ clove of garlic
1 tablespoonful pine nuts
1 small onion, sliced
1 tablespoonful parsley, chopped
½ cup dry white wine

Cut fish into 2-inch slices, having first filleted it. Put three tablespoonfuls of olive oil in an iron pan and cook the onions in it until gently brown. Add the slices of anchovy, parsley, pine nuts and garlic and cook all together five minutes. Then use them as a raft to carry the bits of mackerel, season these with pepper and salt and cook until brown in the oil. Add the wine and cook again very slowly until it is all absorbed. This dish is usually served with a garlic sauce made like a mayonnaise with two cloves of garlic crushed and mingled in. **Pine nuts** (known locally as pinions) are from the large cones of the umbrella pines which grow in great stretches of woodland all along the coast of the Riviera. They are shed in great profusion each autumn and are obtainable for the trouble of picking up, the cones when the nuts have been extracted being used for fuel. No doubt chopped almonds would do as a substitute, but they would be tougher and spikier than the nice little pinions.

Stewed Bream

(Greek and known in Greece as **Plaki**)

Cook a large sliced onion and two chopped dried figs in water with a little salt. When done add the cleaned bream (or any similar sized fish such as bass) and cook gently about ten minutes, or until fish is tender. Lift it out carefully and place in a buttered casserole with the onion, a tablespoonful of chopped parsley, two teaspoonfuls of chopped capers, two chopped leaves of tarragon and thick slices of tomato all over the top. The stewed onion and figs should be mixed with the herbs, pepper and salt, to form a bed for the fish and the tomato above it be dotted with little dabs of butter, and sprinkled with the juice of a lemon. Cook until tomato is soft and gently browned.

Bouillabaisse (Marseilles)

No two recipes for this are alike and even the great masters of cooking quarrel violently as to whether it should be simmered or galloped, include lobster or not, or wine or not. The genuine article, as served locally, has small octopus, shellfish and eel, and enough small red, green, blue and striped fishes in it to make a rainbow. Let's not bother about that version. The thing to remember is that to make a bouillabaise and not a mess you need *firm* fleshed fish, and I don't believe anyone has ever bothered to say that before.

Choose then, sole, eel, turbot, crab or lobster, carp and whiting, or ask the fishmonger about substitutes. Stew in a saucepan a " bouquet garni " of a bayleaf, blade of mace, three cloves, a sprig of fennel, a circle of orange peel, three chopped onions, two carrots, three cloves of garlic, four peppercorns, a twig of thyme and a good spray of parsley, all tied in a muslin bag. Cook for an hour in four cups of water and half a cup of olive oil and two cups of white wine, to get a good start of the fish. Then add the fish, cut up, seasoned with salt, pepper, a grating of nutmeg and a good pinch of saffron, and poach gently until fish is tender but not disintegrated. Possibly five minutes will do for this. Fry some croutons in oil, lay them in a dish, lift out the fish without breaking, throw away your bouquet in the bag and pour the liquid over the fish, having tasted it first for seasoning. This dish may be unadventurous by Mediterranean standards, but it is delicious and the ingredients obtainable anywhere.

Stewed Carp

Begin by preparing what is called a *court bouillon*, the water, wine and herbs as in the previous recipe, plus two branches of celery. When boiled down to half quantity add a carp or a blue trout (cleaned and rolled in muslin), which has been sprinkled with vinegar and oil and left for an hour. Poach gently for ten minutes, lift out carefully and serve on a very hot dish, pouring over it at the very last moment two ounces of sizzling hot butter. Use the same method for *pike and salmon.*

Cod (Salt) Boiled (Italian)

Soak the cod in a dish left under a running tap for not less than eight and up to twenty-four hours to get the salt out of it. In France and Italy it can be bought ready soaked. Use:

1½ lb. soaked cod
3 tablespoonfuls olive oil
1 onion
2 pickled gherkins, chopped
½ lb. green olives, stoned
2 tablespoonfuls sultanas
3 tablespoonfuls flour
2 tablespoonfuls tomato paste
½ pint water
1 tablespoonful capers
1 tablespoonful chopped parsley
2 tablespoonfuls pine nuts or shredded almonds

Skin the soaked fish and cut into three-inch squares. Roll in flour and fry a deep brown in olive oil in an iron pan. Take out and keep hot, then fry onion in the oil, add tomato paste, cook for a moment and add water, gherkin, capers, olives and a good taste of pepper. When blended and thickened return the fish, simmer 15 minutes, test for seasoning, add parsley and serve very hot.

Cod, Fried (Viennese)

3 lb. cod
1 tablespoonful lemon juice
2 tablespoonfuls frying fat
½ teaspoonful basil
1 teaspoonful parsley
2 tablespoonfuls flour for sauce
½ cup sour cream
½ pint water and vinegar mixed
1 tablespoonful flour
2 tablespoonfuls butter
½ teaspoonful rosemary
¼ lb. chopped mushrooms
¾ cup fish stock or water for sauce
1 tablespoonful chopped shallots

Skin the fresh cod and soak in water and vinegar for an hour. Dry, roll in lemon juice, sprinkle with salt and pepper, dip in flour and fry in smoking hot fat until golden brown.

Fry chopped shallots in butter. Add chopped herbs and mushrooms and cook ten minutes. Stir in flour and water, blend well and cook three minutes then add sour cream and fried fish, bring to boil again and serve with butterflies of sliced lemon.

Another Cod Recipe (Venetian)

calls for the same amount of fish cut in pieces. Brown a clove of chopped garlic and two teaspoonfuls of chopped rosemary in olive oil, add a large can of tomatoes, half a cup of dry white wine, a good grating of nutmeg, salt and pepper to taste, and pour all over fish. Cover pan and cook very slowly for an hour, then add half-a-dozen dabs of butter and a grating of cheese with a sprinkle of breadcrumbs and brown in the oven gently until a crisp crust forms on top.

Cod, Grilled

(Also good for fresh tunny)

Lay a slice of fresh fish about two inches thick, in a bath of olive oil, lemon juice, salt and pepper, chopped chives, shallot, fennel, thyme, basil, parsley and a couple of bay leaves. Let it remain for at least four hours, turning occasionally from time to time, to let the delicate flavours penetrate. When needed, remove from the marinade, drain off the oil and grill it gently until crisp and brown. Serve with parsley butter.

Crab Pilaff (Hungarian)

Brown two chopped onions in oil and add a tablespoonful of flour, a chopped and deseeded pimento, chopped thyme, parsley, tarragon, and garlic with half a pound of tomatoes chopped small, and a teaspoonful of saffron. Simmer for five minutes or so then add a pint of fish stock and half a pound of cooked rice not quite soft. When this mixture is boiling lower into it the flesh of two cooked crabs (or two tins of crab) and a teaspoonful of paprika. Cook for another half-hour, test for seasoning and serve with a sprinkle of parsley.

Eel with Sauce Tartare (French)

Get the fishmonger to skin the eel, otherwise it will be a struggle involving salted hands and a pair of pliers. Clean it out and wipe with a cloth. Simmer a "Court bouillon" as for Bouillabaise or carp, for half an hour, then roll the eel into a circle with its tail tucked into its tummy where you removed the intestines and tie it in a piece of muslin to keep its shape.

Cook gently in the liquor for half an hour, then remove it and put aside to cool. Melt 2 ozs. of butter in a saucepan, add two table-spoonfuls of flour and cook for three minutes. Pour on gradually half a pint of the liquor and stir as it boils to get a smooth consistency. Remove from heat and add an egg yolk, then cool the sauce slightly and coat the cooled eel all over with it. Roll eel in bread crumbs, dip carefully into a bowl containing a whole egg beaten up with two teaspoonfuls of olive oil, then sprinkle with a mixture of chopped herbs—tarragon, parsley, chives and onion, and lastly in the crumbs again.

Now have a cupful of olive oil very hot in a large frying pan and fry the eel quickly until it is brown and crisp.

You may think this is an awful long-winded way of cooking an eel when they can be bought plain boiled. But just try it and you will say that it is the best fish dish you ever tasted. Serve *Tartare Sauce* with it, piled up in the eel's inner circle on a very hot dish. Tartare is, as you know, mayonnaise made with egg yolk, oil and vinegar, with chopped tarragon, parsley and capers worked into it.

Fish in Aspic (Swedish)

2½ lbs. firm fish, mackerel, eel or turbot. Prepare a court bouillon as above and cook half an hour. Cut up the fish into neat strips and poach gently in the liquor about ten minutes or less. Cool in liquor. Soak 2 ozs. of gelatine in cold water then dilute with 2 pints of hot fish stock until all is melted, beat in two egg whites to clear the stock and bring slowly to boiling point in saucepan, stirring all the time. When it boils stop stirring and allow it to simmer gently for about twenty minutes and form a scummy crust. All the particles in the liquor will get poached into the egg-white and the aspic in consequence be crystal clear. Strain through muslin and season highly. Decorate the bottom of a mould with fancy shapes of egg, radish, tomato, little shrimps, sprigs of dill or anything else colourful and edible and pour over this some of the cool stock. When set in a jelly, lower in the fish carefully in a pattern, do some more egg-and-tomato fancy-work round the sides and fill up with stock. Chill until it is quite jellied and turn out to serve cold with mayonnaise. A good summer luncheon dish. The identical liquor with meat instead of fish, cleared in the same way and with the meat cut into neat shapes and placed in the decorated mould makes equally good *steak or veal, pigeon or chicken in aspic.* The herbs are the same in either case.

Frogs Legs, Fried (French)

Soak the frogs legs in water two hours, then dry and flour them. *Saute* in butter with chopped parsley, dill, chives, shallots, and when brown sprinkle with pepper and lemon juice.

Another way is to marinade the legs (four pairs for each person) in white wine, onion, chopped chives, tarragon, parsley and bay leaf, salt and pepper, and let them remain in this two hours. Then flour and fry as before.

Gurnets with Green Sauce

Slash the fish across twice to facilitate cooking, dip them in oil, sprinkle with a little salt, pepper, and nutmeg, then with buttered crumbs and grill them. Meanwhile chop very finely three tarragon leaves, a teaspoonful each of chives, parsley, capers, chervil and gherkins. Mingle these with two tablespoonfuls of thick cream, two egg yolks, the juice of half a lemon and two tablespoonfuls of olive oil, added alternately and gradually to prevent curdling. Chill and serve the cold sauce with the hot gurnets. It is also very good with cold salmon, trout, jellied eel or carp.

Halibut or Haddock, Baked (Italian)

1 slice of fish an inch thick for each person
1 potato for each person
1 medium onion, chopped
1 tablespoonful chopped parsley
4 chopped anchovy fillets
1 minced clove of garlic
1 sprig chopped dill
½ cup olive oil

Butter a fireproof dish, slice half the potatoes into it, sprinkle with half the other ingredients, including oil and seasoning, lay in the fish pieces and cover with the other half of potatoes, onion and herbs, pouring oil over last. Bake in a good oven half an hour until crisp and brown.

Herrings (Swedish Fashion)

Soak some herrings in water overnight then bang them on a board to loosen the backbones. Slit, split, clean and fillet them. Lay on each fillet a mixture of chopped capers, chervil, parsley, dill, shallots, lemon juice and seasoning, roll and place in a flat dish. Cover with a mixture of vinegar, oil, salt, pepper and sugar, and leave overnight to get mellowed. They are then eaten with green salad.

Herrings as Hors d'œuvre (French)

Get some plain smoked herrings, skin them and remove the heads, tails and fins. Soak them in milk for two hours to remove some of the salt, then dry them and place in a casserole with a layer of herbs and a layer of herrings. Herbs should include chopped parsley, bay leaves, thyme, celery, dill, chervil, juniper berries, onion, and carrot. Pour over the fish and herbs a cup of white wine and two tablespoonfuls of olive oil, cover the casserole with its lid and leave the fish to marinate for four days. After this they may be removed to a flat dish minus the herbs, sprinkled with slices of onion soaked in vinegar and garnished with sprigs of fennel or dill.

Mackerel, Stuffed (Armenian)

Cut off head of each mackerel and clean without opening the belly. Snap spine at tail end and roll fish heavily with palm of hand to loosen backbone. It should then pull out. If any flesh comes with it scrape it off bones and use it mixed with the following stuffing: 2 onions, 1 carrot, a dozen green gooseberries, ½ teaspoonful tarragon, 2 teaspoonfuls parsley, ½ teaspoonful allspice, 2 tablespoonfuls pine nuts or almonds, a handful of bread crumbs soaked in milk and wrung out, plenty of salt and pepper. Chop all these finely, together with any fish bits, and stuff back into mackerel's interior with the handle of a wooden spoon. Dip fish in egg-and-oil batter and fry in deep fat or oil.

Matelote Bourgeoise (French). Mixed Fish

3 lbs. mixed fish, eel, carp, cod, whiting, fresh haddock and hake, all cut into even strips about one inch by three, and poach gently for ten minutes in a "court bouillon" similar to that for bouillabaise, except that no water is used and a whole bottle of cheap red wine

instead, Fry a pound of onions gently in butter, in a large pan. Add 2 tablespoonfuls flour and cook three minutes, thin down with a cupful of the fish liquor strained, let the flour swell then add another cup of liquor, stirring until it is a smooth sauce and if still too thick add more liquid; it should be the consistency of cream-of-tomato soup. Add ½ lb. of cleaned and peeled mushrooms, a pinch of powdered mace and the fish strips and cook very gently about ten minutes until all is blended well together. Serve in a large flat dish with fingers of fried bread and fried shrimps around. This is a splendid and original dish for a *fork supper*.

Mullet, Baked (Italian)

2 lb. of red mullet cleaned and washed
2 tablespoonfuls olive oil
2 tablespoonfuls flour
2 tablespoonfuls tomato purée
1 teaspoonful parsley
1 small onion
¼ teaspoonful thyme
¼ teaspoonful marjoram
1 crushed bay leaf
½ clove crushed garlic

Flour the mullet and put in a fireproof pan with the oil, cooking gently until done on both sides. Add all the chopped herbs, etc., with a good seasoning of salt and pepper and the *purée* diluted with half a cup of red wine. Cook in the oven another ten minutes and serve very hot, lightly sprinkled with chopped chives.

All fish for baking should be very fresh or it will not be firm.

Mullet en Papilotte (Greek)

Cooked in a bag.

Clean and salt the mullets and in the cavity which contained the intestines put a roll of lean bacon. Dip each fish in olive oil and sprinkle it with salt and pepper, then place on an oblong of greased paper. Fold this over several times at side and ends, lay the packages on an oven dish and bake about twenty minutes. When done, remove papers, lay fish on a hot dish, and sprinkle with chopped sage and parsley and a squeeze of lemon juice, Sage and fish is very unusual, but in this case very good.

Mullet Farci en Croute (French)

Stuffed in a crust.

Take one mullet for each two people, clean them, remove head, tail and fins and fillet them. Prepare a stuffing of shrimps, mushrooms, shallots, mussels (opened in a pan, shaken over the fire for a few minutes and their juice strained into the mixture with them), half a glass of white wine, parsley, lemon juice and two leaves of tarragon. All herbs should be finely chopped with the shallot and the mushrooms, mussels and shrimps coarsely chopped, the whole well mixed into a paste, a layer of which is laid on each half mullet and sprinkled with a few drops of oil.

Prepare a good short crust and cut into oblongs twice the width and rather more than the length of the mullet fillets; shape again in the pastry the missing heads and tails and put some stuffing inside to keep them in shape. Wet the edges of the pastry and press together, making it look as much like a fish as possible. Reform the gills behind the head with knife slits and use currants for eyes. Prick with a skewer in imitation of scales. Place on a greased baking dish or Pyrex oven dish and bake half an hour in a moderate oven, about 350°. These are delicious either hot or cold.

Mussels Mariniere (French)

Mussels must be absolutely fresh. If one has a shell which is even slightly ajar discard it, because, like an oyster in the same state, it is dead.

When wanted for cooking, scrub them thoroughly in several waters to remove the sand. Now place them in a saucepan with a cup of white wine and onion, carrot, garlic, herbs and seasoning—in fact make a court bouillon with no water and place in it the mussels, about half a pint for each person. Put lid on pan and place over heat, the more heat the better, until all the shells are opened, The mussels are then done. Lay them on a deep dish, remove the top shell of each and pour the court bouillon through a strainer over them.

Or having cooked them, put an ounce of butter in a pan, add a tablespoonful of flour, and when it has bubbled a few minutes, thin it down, mixing in each addition of the bouillon very gradually until you have used two cups. Remove the mussels from both shells and add to the sauce which should be quite thick. Put it on buttered scallop shells for each person or small pyrex dishes, cover with buttered crumbs, and bake in the oven until crisp and brown. See that each dish gets a fair portion of mussels and just before serving sprinkle with chopped parsley and chives.

Oysters Marinées (French)

Have the oysters opened by the fishmonger and carry them home in a dish to save the liquor. Chop finely 2 tablespoonfuls shallots, 1 teaspoonful thyme, the same of marjoram, 2 blades of tarragon and 3 of lemon verbena, and chop some hard-boiled eggs not so finely, keeping yolks and whites separate. Put a layer of herbs, shallots and egg white, mixed, on the bottom of a glass bowl, next lay the oysters on it, sprinkle them with the egg yolks rubbed through a coarse sieve, some oil and lemon juice, paprika and chopped tarragon leaves. Put in the refrigerator for several hours before serving.

That was cold oysters, the next one is *hot oysters* and very simple. Take 2 large flat mushrooms for each person and sprinkle with salt some hours before cooking, to bring out the flavour. When ready to cook, place three oysters, with their liquor, on each mushroom, which must be the open-faced kind, sprinkle each with lemon juice, salt, pepper, cayenne, a teaspoonful of parsley to each four mushrooms and one of tarragon to each eight. Scatter crumbs over all and dabs of butter on top. Cook under the grill or in a moderate oven until the crumbs are brown and mushrooms soft with the combined juice of oysters, mushrooms and lemon making a celestial gravy.

Paella (Spanish Fish Stew)

Cook a mixture of fish, without bones, in cider (or half water and half white wine), and let it include as many kinds as possible—shrimps, sole, carp, lobster, whiting, anything at all—and mix it with ½ lb. of hot boiled rice. Add chopped parsley, tarragon, and a little dill, olive oil, pepper, salt, cayenne and paprika with saffron and powdered mace. Cook all together a few moments and serve very hot.

Patties (Austrian)

½ lb. salt pork	*1 tablespoonful parsley*
1 chopped onion	*1 lb. potatoes*
½ cup milk	*1 cup bread-crumbs*
1½ lb. fish	*Mixed herbs*
2 tablespoonfuls fat	

Cut the pork and fish into pieces and put through the mincing machine. Boil the potatoes and mash them. Mix all with the onion, which was previously fried in the fat, the bread-crumbs, milk, parsley, marjoram, and a little lemon thyme all chopped, seasoning, and a dash of nutmeg. Mix well and make into flat patties. Dip into egg then into crumbs and brush with melted fat. Bake in a hot oven about 15 minutes. Fish may be of any kind, cooked or uncooked.

Salmon

There is no way better than plain boiled in a Court Bouillon as for Bouillabaise served with Hollandaise or tartare sauce as in the eel recipe. Let it cool in the liquor and serve with a green salad.

Baked Sole

Prepare a large sole, about two pounds or an allowance of about half a pound per head of smaller ones. Clean and remove the black skin. Put two tablespoonfuls of butter in the bottom of a fireproof dish with parsley and onion, and half a teaspoonful each of chopped tarragon and thyme. Place the sole on this, sprinkle with more parsley and onion, pour over it half a glass of dry white wine, sprinkle with crumbs, dot with another ounce of butter in small pieces and bake half an hour in a medium oven. Put under the grill for a few minutes before serving if not brown enough.

Fillets of Sole or Plaice can be treated in just the same way.

Sole à la Creme

is fillets of sole poached very gently in our old friend the Court Bouillon, then removed and kept hot while you boil the liquid fast and reduce it to about half a pint. Pour this through muslin into a clean pan, add a cupful of cream and a pinch of paprika and boil up again, adding a walnut of butter and a teaspoonful of chopped tarragon before pouring it over the fillets and serving.

Trout

Treat as advised for salmon and serve with a teaspoonful of chopped fennel in the sauce.

Turbot

The classic method is again to poach in the Court Bouillon, then serve with caper sauce.

Whiting

Use the baked sole recipe exactly.

Grilled Whiting (Venetian)

Clean and wash the fish, one small one for each person. Leave them in a deep dish soaking in olive oil, lemon juice, salt, pepper, chopped tarragon and rosemary for three hours. Grill them for about ten minutes each side, sprinkling occasionally with the oil mixture as they are cooking.

MEAT

Beefsteak Cacciatora (Italian)

1 thick rump steak
2 tablespoonfuls cooking sherry
½ clove crushed garlic
1 tablespoonful tomato purée
1 tablespoonful olive oil
1 small glass red wine
½ teaspoonful fennel seeds

Fry steak in oil and season well. Remove from pan and keep hot. Pour sherry and red wine into pan, scraping well to loosen gravy, cook until thick and much reduced then add garlic, tomato *purée* and fennel seeds. Cook another minute and serve steak with the gravy poured over it.

Beefsteak Florentine

Treat precisely as advised for grilled whiting.

Beef Olives

There is a good recipe for these tasty morsels in *The Reluctant Cook*, therefore I will not repeat it.

Beef Stew with Fennel (Italian)

3 lb. shin of beef
2 branches chopped celery
1 small can tomato purée
1 tablespoonful parsley, chopped
1 tablespoonful flour
1 tablespoonful butter
¼ lb. chopped bacon
1 large chopped onion
2 cloves garlic
1 teaspoonful fennel seeds
1 cup red wine
2 tablespoonfuls olive oil

Cook the onion, celery and bacon in the olive oil and butter, add the cut-up beef, season well and brown slowly. Add wine and cook gently until it is absorbed, sprinkle with the flour, add the tomato *purée* and enough water to cover all. Put lid on pan and cook slowly two hours or until tender. Add the garlic, fennel seeds and parsley, cook another ten minutes, test for seasoning and serve very hot.

Cutlets en Papillotes

See *The Reluctant Cook*.

Grilled Chops with Herbs

Rub the chops with a cut clove of garlic. And remember that in all recipes mentioning garlic it is optional. You may use shallot if you prefer it that way. But it won't taste the same.

Melt an ounce of butter in a little pan and mix in it one teaspoonful of parsley and half each of tarragon, marjoram and thyme, all finely chopped and seasoned highly with salt, pepper and a grating of nutmeg. Smear a liberal coating of this on both sides of each chop, press them into fine bread crumbs and grill over moderate heat or fry gently in a pan.

Goulash (Hungarian)

3 lb. shin of beef
1 lb. onions
2 teaspoonfuls paprika
1 tablespoonful flour
¼ lb. fat
1 tablespoonful vinegar
2 cups stock
1 teaspoonful each carraway seeds and chopped marjoram

Fry the sliced onions in the fat. Add the cubed meat, paprika, vinegar, herbs, stock and seasoning. Cook slowly three hours or until tender, then thicken with flour, test for seasoning and serve.

Ham Boiled with Parsley (French)

Prepare a Court Bouillon as for fish, but include a calves' foot and a few veal bones to make jelly. Put into this a small ham, or, if expense is a consideration, about six pounds of collar bacon. Cook until quite tender and almost falling to pieces. Remove to a large bowl, remove the bones, cut up all the meat coarsely, mixing fat and lean together, and reduce the stock in which it was cooked by at least half by continuing boiling. Strain it over the ham, add a crushed clove of garlic, a tablespoonful of chopped parsley, a saltspoonful of powdered mace, pepper to taste, and a sherry-glassful of white wine and mix all together thoroughly. Put aside in a cool place to set and turn out when wanted. It is an excellent dish for a large party, served with a green salad.

Ham with Caper (Italian)

Make a marinade as for grilled whiting, but add half a glass of red wine and a teaspoonful of parsley and soak thick slices of ham, one for each person, in it about twelve hours, turning occasionally. Melt two ounces of butter in a pan and brown the ham in it. Remove meat, keep hot and add a tablespoonful of flour to pan, add the strained marinade, boil well, return the ham to pan, add a tablespoonful of tomato paste and a cupful of stock with half a crushed clove of garlic or two shallots. Cover pan and cook very gently one hour. Add two tablespoonfuls capers just before serving.

Kabobs or Shishkabobs (Armenian)

(Originating with the mountain folk of the Caucasus, who, during their wanderings would kill wild game, stick it on a sword, and roast it over the camp fire.)

Marinate small slices of lamb overnight in sherry, oil, onion, marjoram, and parsley, then string on a skewer with buttered mushrooms, split kidneys and half tomatoes alternating. Grill and serve on their silver skewers.

Lamb (Misov Pagla). Armenian Recipe

2 lb. shoulder of lamb, cut up
1 lb. green beans
¼ lb. butter or oil for frying
½ lb. sliced onions
2 tablespoonfuls chopped dill
2 teaspoonfuls paprika

Brown the meat in casserole, add sliced onions and brown, add beans cut up, dill, paprika and plenty of pepper and salt. Put in enough stock to cover and bake gently until meat is done and stock reduced by half.

Lamb Stew (Italian)

2 lb. shoulder of lamb, cubed
3 tablespoonfuls olive oil
2 cloves chopped garlic
1 teaspoonful grated lemon peel
2 tablespoonfuls wine vinegar
6 chopped anchovy fillets
2 oz. butter
1 tablespoonful fennel seeds
1 tablespoonful flour
½ pint stock

Brown the meat in the oil and butter, add anchovies, garlic, fennel seeds, lemon peel and vinegar with salt and pepper, and cook until vinegar is absorbed. Sprinkle in flour, mixing well, then add stock. Cover and stew an hour, slowly.

Fried Liver (Venetian Style)

Fry thin slices of calves liver, remove and keep hot, then fry half a pound of sliced onions, a crushed clove of garlic, and two large tomatoes. Lay a layer of liver in a casserole, then a layer of the onion, then a layer of chopped parsley, thyme, basil, marjoram, carrot, mushroom, with seasoning of salt and pepper, spice, and a sprinkle of lemon juice. Another layer of liver, another of onion and garlic and another of herbs and so on until dish is full. Pour over all two tablespoonfuls of oil and two of vinegar. Cook very slowly for an hour. Just before serving sprinkle in a little flour to thicken and let it come back to boiling point for a minute or two.

Liver

is also quite good alternated with a stuffing of plain boiled onions and rubbed sage, well seasoned with salt and pepper and cooked with strips of fat bacon in a casserole.

Ox Tongue, Stewed (Dutch)

Cook the tongue very slowly until the bones come out readily, about three hours. Skin and remove small bones. Slice a pound of tomatoes and put into the liquor with a tablespoonful parsley, three cloves, a bay leaf and a quarter pound of sliced mushrooms. Cook all together gently ten minutes, until reduced a little, thicken with a tablespoonful of flour slaked in cold water, boil up again, add pepper and salt to taste and serve tongue hot with the sauce poured over it.

Pork Chops, Modena Fashion (Italian)

1 chop per person
1 teaspoonful sage
½ cup dry white wine
1 teaspoonful rosemary
1 tablespoonful chopped shallot

Mix all the chopped herbs and shallot with pepper and salt and sprinkle on both sides of each chop. Put chops in a shallow pan with just enough water to cover them. Cook slowly until it has evaporated and they will then brown. Turn them occasionally then when tender and well browned add the wine, cook for a moment to loosen the good gravy on sides of pan and serve.

The Japanese sprinkle their pork chops with carraway seeds before frying.

The Viennese cut the pork into stewing pieces and cook in salted water with a cup of vinegar, 6 peppercorns, celery root, onion, parsley root, 2 sage leaves and a bay leaf and a quarter teaspoonful of carraway seeds, and cook until tender. Then pour the strained gravy over it and grate a root of fresh horseradish over all, surrounding the meat with plain boiled potatoes.

Pork Fillet à la Colbert

Have a thin slice of pork fillet for each person. Take a tender young cabbage and pour boiling water over the separated leaves to remove the strong flavour, then lay on each a slice of pork which has been banged with a wooden spoon to spread and make it bendable. Scatter each with salt, pepper and a *few* carraway seeds, then spread with the following mixture—

quarter pound of mushrooms, one large onion, one tablespoonful parsley all chopped and fried. Roll up and wind a bit of cotton round each leaf with its contents. Place side by side on a baking dish containing a little stock and baste from time to time until cooked (about an hour at 375°).

Pot Roast (Viennese)

3 lb. chunky beef, silverside or a similar bit
2 cups stock
A dozen peppercorns
Half a celery root
1 onion
1 bay leaf
Sprig of thyme
4 tablespoonfuls fat
1 cup red wine
1 parsley root
1 carrot
1 turnip
¼ teaspoonful pudding spice

Fry the roots and onion in an iron saucepan in the fat. Add the meat after rubbing it all over with vinegar and brown well on all sides. Add the stock and wine, peppercorns and herbs and simmer very, very slowly for four hours, adding more stock if necessary. Serve with the liquid strained over meat.

Veal Fricandeau (French)

Cook in an iron pan in butter three rashers of bacon, half a pound of onions, half-pound carrots, a little chopped parsley, thyme, rosemary bay leaf, two cloves, and three peppercorns.

Then add three pounds of leg of veal (or more) with enough stock to cover and some salt. Cook very slowly with the lid on for three hours, when it should be tender enough to cut with a spoon. Sieve the liquor and pour over meat.

Veal chops are exactly the same, except that the chops are well browned in the pan before you add the herbs and vegetables. Cook for only half an hour very slowly. Rub vegetables through a sieve over the chops on a dish.

Veal Stew is cubes of shoulder veal browned in oil in the pan with chopped parsley, thyme, garlic, marjoram, salt, pepper and a cupful of dry white wine stewed with it until it is all evaporated. Add a large can of tomatoes and all their juice with salt and pepper and stew very gently about 1½ hours or until tender. Gravy should be thick and rich, no further treatment is necessary, serve all together.

Venison Fillets (Flemish)

Take one slice of venison (well hung) for each person and marinate them 24 hours in the following mixture—a tumbler of wine vinegar, one of red wine, 3 tablespoonfuls olive oil, a bay leaf, a branch of thyme, a branch of parsley, three tarragon leaves, three chopped shallots, two juniper berries, salt and pepper, and a piece of stick cinnamon. Boil all this for five minutes and when cold pour it over the venison slices in a deep dish. Baste the slices or turn them over occasionally during the 24 hours steeping, then wipe each one dry with a cloth and fry them in butter. Keep hot on a dish and into the buttery pan pour enough of the marinade mixture to make gravy, thicken with flour and add a tablespoonful of brandy at the last moment. Pour the gravy over the slices and serve with red currant jelly and boiled chestnuts.

POULTRY AND GAME

Chicken Cacciatora

Cut up a chicken and treat as for Beef Cacciatora.

Chicken Gumbo. See page 75

Chicken with Rice (German)

1 chicken stuffed with thyme, parsley and lemon forcemeat
2 pints of stock
One onion stuck with three cloves
Bouquet garni
Juice of one lemon
½ lb. rice
½ teaspoonful saffron
2 egg yolks

Bring the stock to the boil then put in the rice, the chicken, the herbs tied with cotton, saffron, salt and pepper and the onion. Cook very gently until rice is soft and chicken cooked. Remove bird to a dish and stir into pan two egg yolks and the strained juice of a lemon after removing bouquet garni. Pour rice, etc., over chicken on dish.

Game Stew (American)

Take a cut-up rabbit, plus a pigeon, an old partridge and a quail, or any other game obtainable. Joint them and dip in flour then brown in hot olive oil. Fry also two pounds tomatoes, one pound onions, and two teaspoonfuls parsley with two cloves of chopped garlic, then put in a large pan with the mixed game, four diced carrots, ten peppercorns, three cloves, salt, a teaspoonful of chopped thyme and marjoram mixed and two pints of stock. Simmer slowly until tender.

Gibelotte of Rabbit (Belgian)

Disjoint a young rabbit and marinate it overnight in the usual mixture of red wine, vinegar, thyme, marjoram, parsley and chopped shallot. When you remove the rabbit this mixture may be put in the refrigerator and used again and again for other meat. After removing from the liquid dip the rabbit joints in flour and fry to a good golden brown and put them in an iron saucepan with ½ lb. of prunes soaked overnight in water, one cup of red wine and enough of the marinade to cover the whole. Season with salt, pepper and a dash of nutmeg, and simmer very slowly until rabbit is tender. Serve with red currant jelly.

The Italians make the same dish in the same way but add pine nuts and seedless raisins to the stew instead of prunes. When tender add 2 tablespoonfuls tomato paste, 6 chopped olives, a dozen chopped capers and a dessertspoonful of sugar to the gravy.

Guisado of Hare (Spanish)

Wipe and cut up a hare, carefully preserving the liver, heart and blood. Brown a large onion in butter, flour and brown the hare and put all into a casserole with seasoning, a teaspoonful of chopped parsley, half a teaspoonful each of chopped sage and marjoram, three red peppers de-seeded, two crushed cloves of garlic, a quarter pound of diced bacon, a quarter teaspoonful of pudding spice, and enough stock and red wine (in equal proportions) to cover the whole. Simmer very slowly in the oven with the lid on, about three hours, or until the meat is tender. Mix the blood and chopped liver with vinegar, mix and boil up for three minutes.

Gumbo (Creole)

1 boiling fowl or large rabbit
2 dozen oysters and their liquor, but if in a locality where oysters are expensive this ingredient may be omitted
½ lb. tomatoes, sliced
½ pod of de-seeded red pepper or pimento, pork fat, flour, cayenne, parsley, thyme, bay leaf
½ lb. knuckle of ham
¼ lb. rice
4 cups okra
2 pints water

Cut up the chicken or rabbit. Dredge with seasoned flour and fry in a deep pot with the pork fat, the onion, ham, parsley, thyme, tomatoes, cayenne pepper, pimento or red pepper, okra sliced (either freshly cooked or out of a can, according to which country you live in) and when nicely browned put in the water and the oyster liquor. Cook very slowly with the lid on until the meat is done, then add the oysters, any additional seasoning necessary and a cupful of cream. Re-heat for a few minutes and serve with rice boiled separately and carefully so that every grain is separate. It is possible to buy tinned oysters so that if the fresh ones are out of season *Gumbo* can still be achieved. Tinned pimentos are also obtainable.

Hare St. Hubert (Italian)

1 hare, jointed
2 chopped onions
2 branches celery, chopped
2 sage leaves
½ teaspoonful rosemary
4 juniper berries
2 teaspoonfuls grated orange rind
¼ pint wine vinegar
3 tablespoonfuls olive oil
2 carrots, sliced
2 cloves
1 teaspoonful thyme
½ teaspoonful marjoram
1 clove sliced garlic
¾ pint dry red wine
½ pint stock

Put the olive oil in a thick saucepan and brown the sliced vegetables. Add the herbs and garlic and cook a few minutes. Add the wine and vinegar, bring to the boil and boil one minute, Cool, add the hare and let it remain overnight. Next day brown the hare pieces in a frying pan in oil, add the vegetables from the marinade and when they are brown add some of the liquid. Each time it becomes dry add more until it is all used. Cover pan and cook very slowly until hare is tender. Add the orange rind and serve with red currant jelly.

Mexican Rabbit Mole

Cook a tender rabbit, disjointed, in a little salted water until not quite tender. Remove from pan and after dipping in flour, fry golden brown in bacon fat. Prepare a sauce with these ingredients—1 green pepper de-seeded, 2 tablespoonfuls almonds or pine nuts, 2 tablespoonfuls seeded raisins, 1 sliced garlic clove, 1 medium sliced onion.

Olla Podrida (Spanish)

Clean a rabbit and cut into pieces. Boil for an hour, slowly, in a quart of water with pepper and salt added. Cook together in another pan, onions, red peppers, carrots, cauliflower, one blade of mace, two dozen black olives, chopped sage, thyme, parsley, and chopped garlic. When all is nearly ready put a dozen oysters and their liquor into the rabbit broth and serve all together on a dish, rabbit in the middle, vegetables round.

Escabescia of Partridges (Spanish)

Heat some oil in a pan and brown two young partridges. Add to the pan a clove of chopped garlic, a bay leaf, ¼ teaspoonful pudding spice, a tablespoonful tomato paste, chopped thyme and marjoram, a little chopped rosemary and a chopped onion. Brown all of this a little with the addition of bread crumbs for thickening. Add enough stock to cover everything, put on the lid and simmer very gently about twenty minutes or until birds are tender. Take birds out and keep warm while you boil the liquid to reduce the quantity, then strain it over the birds after tasting for flavour.

Pigeons, Braised (German)

2 fat young pigeons
2 tablespoonfuls cream
1 dessertspoonful flour
½ teaspoonful marjoram
1 tablespoonful minced fat bacon
2 eggs
2 tablespoonfuls butter
1 teaspoonful parsley
½ teaspoonful thyme
1 tablespoonful bread crumbs

Melt the butter in a thick pan. Brown in it the minced liver and gizzards, bacon, bread crumbs, flour, parsley, thyme, marjoram, with a pinch of nutmeg, salt and pepper. Braise the birds in this until tender. Remove and keep hot, then thicken the mixture with the two raw eggs and cream, mixed together for a few moments but never actually boiled. Put the pigeons back into it for a few moments and serve with it poured over them inside a border of stewed chestnuts.

Quails in Vine Leaves (Egyptian)

Fill quails with parsley and thyme stuffing. Grease the birds with butter and roll each in a large vine leaf, then wrap each round with two long strips of bacon fat and roll a bit of cotton round to hold it all together. Pack them into a tin and cook for fifteen minutes. Serve on squares of toast with their gravy poured over, and a garnish of watercress. Vine leaves and all are eaten; just remove the cotton before serving.

Quails (Greek Fashion)

Brown the birds in an iron pan with butter. Add chopped celery, a small onion, parsley, sage, and garlic, all finely chopped and lastly, enough red wine to cover. Cook gently about fifteen minutes. Test for seasoning, add a knob of butter and a tablespoonful of cream, and serve.

Rabbit with Rice (Mexican)

1 tender rabbit
1 de-seeded green pepper
1 medium onion
1½ cups unpolished rice
1 tablespoonful olive oil
1 bay leaf
1 small glass sherry
¼ lb. bacon
1 small can pimentos
1 clove of garlic
1 dozen black olives
1 teaspoonful parsley, minced
2 cloves
¼ stick cinnamon

Fry the onion and garlic in a heavy pan with

the oil, add the cut-up rabbit and chopped bacon, then, when brown, add the parsley, bay leaf, cloves and cinnamon all in a piece of muslin. Add the rice and enough stock to cover the meat, season with pepper and salt and simmer very slowly until all the liquid is absorbed and the rabbit is tender. Add the sherry, olives and pimentos sliced in strips, simmer another five minutes and serve very hot.

Rabbit, Sweet-Sour (American)

This is the same recipe as Hare St. Hubert, which see, but finish with this sauce:

Melt two tablespoonfuls brown sugar in a small saucepan and add two tablespoonfuls vinegar, two tablespoonfuls seeded raisins chopped, and two tablespoonfuls pine nuts or almonds. Cook all together for a few moments and serve instead of red currant jelly.

Roman Pie

Take one pound of rabbit meat and one pound of veal trimmings, mix with a few pieces of cowheel, a teaspoonful of parsley, and ¼ teaspoonful each of marjoram and thyme. Roll all the meat pieces in flour. Thickly grease a pudding basin and sprinkle with vermicelli, then line with pastry. Pack into it the cut-up rabbit and veal with ¼ lb. chopped bacon, two ounces of boiled macaroni, a chopped shallot, a tablespoonful of grated cheese, two tablespoonfuls of cream, the chopped herbs and cow-heel and a good dusting of salt and pepper. When all is packed into the crust pour over it half a cupful of water and fix on the pastry lid. Cover with several layers of buttered paper and bake in a moderate oven at least two hours; it will not harm if it is there three hours. Turn out on a hot dish and serve with parsley sauce.

Soufflé of Game

Mince any left-over rabbit, chicken, pheasant or partridge, about two breakfast-cups, and mix with ½ tablespoonful chopped parsley and ½ teaspoonful each of chopped thyme and marjoram, mixed with a teaspoonful grated lemon peel. Put 3 oz. butter in a pan and when melted add 3 tablespoonfuls flour, mix and dilute with ½ pint milk, cooking until thick and smooth. Season highly with salt and pepper, beat in 3 egg yolks and the meat-and-herb mixture, then prepare a soufflé mould with greased paper round the outside, reaching well above the mould, and a plentiful lubrication of butter on the inside of the mould. Beat the 3 egg whites very stiff and fold into the mixture gently, then bake 30–40 minutes in an oven at 375° and serve at once. Repeat *at once* as it deflates very rapidly.

SALADS AND VEGETABLES

HERBS in a salad are not only a garnish but a necessity, and once you have concocted a salad with chopped fennel, little leaves of basil, tarragon and rocket, sprigs of parsley and dill and even the despised garlic, you will never be able to look a plain unaccompanied lettuce in the face again. When you become a really accomplished salad-mixer you will think nothing of the above herbs and go adventuring with the buds of black-currant bushes (very delicious), young daisy leaves, nasturtium flowers and leaves, young borage leaves and vine tendrils. You may object that vine tendrils and black currants and such nonsense are no herbs and therefore have no part in this treatise. To which I reply, " Look at the quotation heading, Chapter One. What was good enough for our fathers should be good enough for us," and you might have a look at the Ruskin quotation on the flyleaf while you're about it.

In addition to the herbs and saladings the ingredients with which they are dressed are important. The vinegar must be the best wine vinegar and the oil the best olive, which really *tastes* of olives, not that sticky and anonymous material which passes as salad oil all too often. There is only one thing which is more exquisite for this purpose than good olive oil and that is good walnut oil which really tastes of walnuts. But where to get it? That is another thing.

There is an old chateau near Grenoble—I will not be more precise than that—and spread all around in the sunshine are its vines and its walnuts, the products of which are exceptional and never leave the estate. The nuts are crushed and the oil stored, and when I want to make a salad I use it in great quantity because there is always plenty more—which applies also to the wine. But commercially I do not know. It is made where it is made because it was always so. No one knows or ever *did* know whether it was a paying crop. It is the oil par excellence for a salad, and as one must have salads one naturally grows and crushes and uses the perfect oil and the rest of the world uses what they must.

In your case presumably you must use olive. But get the best. And do leave the dressing of a salad until the last minute. You may wash and swing your saladings and herbs dry an hour before if you like, but leave the actual mixing until just before eating, or the oil and vinegar will penetrate the delicate green leaves and make them brown and transparent and exceedingly unappetising. That is for green salads, but with vegetable salads it is different, and you may prepare them hours in advance if necessary and allow the ingredients to mellow and get to know each other amiably; a process which brings out the delicate flavour of the herbs.

Artichoke Salad

Cook two dozen small artichokes (having first cut off their tough tips and outer leaves and thrown them into lemon juice and water to keep the colour) in a mixture of wine vinegar, 2 tablespoonfuls, and 3 cups white wine, 2 tablespoonfuls olive oil, juice of 2 lemons, 3 bay leaves, 3 cloves, a branch each of fennel and celery, thyme, a bay leaf, and a few coriander seeds. It sounds a complicated mixture, but once you get into the habit of having all these on hand it is no worse than adding salt and pepper, and this marinade in which you boil the artichokes will serve for meat or fish if you keep it. Cook them for twenty minutes then leave them in the mixture to get cold. They may be stored in it for a month if need be. When wanted drain them and toss them in fresh oil and lemon juice.

Aubergines à la Provençale

Peel six aubergines, sprinkle with salt and leave for an hour to get rid of excess water and with it bitterness, fry them both sides in hot olive oil and remove to a flat dish. Fry three large sliced tomatoes in the oil to a *purée* with half a tablespoonful of parsley, two leaves of tarragon and two chopped anchovies. Put a spoonful of this *purée* on each slice of cold aubergine, arrange a ring of anchovy on top of this, a black olive in the ring of anchovy, a sprinkle of lemon and oil over all and a pinch of chopped parsley to crown each. Chill before serving.

Beans (Green)

Boil in salted water very quickly and sprinkle with chives, chervil, parsley and young onions, all chopped plus oil and lemon juice. Serve cold.

An alternative dressing is chopped capers, garlic, tarragon, parsley, tomatoes, and a sprinkle of oil and vinegar.

Beans, Broad (French)

Cook quickly in salted water with parsley and savory. Drain well. Prepare a sauce with butter and flour and two chopped rashers of fat bacon, salt and pepper it, add a teaspoonful of chopped parsley and about four leaves of chopped savory, some of the water in which the beans were cooked, the beans themselves, mix gently and serve.

Red Cabbage (Alsatian)

Blanch the cabbage (shredded fine) in boiling water for a minute to remove strong flavour. Drain it and press dry, then toss in oil and wine vinegar in which chopped lemon balm and chervil, salt, pepper and three crushed juniper berries have been blended. Chill before serving.

Another Red Cabbage Recipe

Blanch a shredded red cabbage as above then marinate it in tarragon vinegar for an hour. Take a cupful of sour milk or cream, the mashed yolks of four hard-boiled eggs, salt, pepper, lemon juice, chopped chervil, tarragon and fennel and mix the cabbage in it. Let it stand for an hour, then decorate it with sprigs of celery of dill and wheels of cucumber with the rind on.

Carrottes Marineés (French)

Cook as many carrots as you need in a Court Bouillon as for salmon or bouillabaise.

but mix a dessertspoonful of curry with some of the liquid before boiling. When tender let the carrots cool in the mixture.

Cauliflower

when eaten cold as a salad is dressed while still warm with two tablespoonfuls of oil to a dessertspoonful of wine vinegar and sprinkled with chopped chervil, parsley and chives.

Cos Lettuce Salad

The best and crispest kind of lettuce is a cos. The French like the large black-seeded cos known as romaine, but I prefer a small self-hearting variety known as Winter Density which grows just as well in summer as in winter and tastes deliciously of walnuts. Discard just the outer leaves after washing it and after putting oil and vinegar, a little salt and a half teaspoonful of fine sugar into a bowl which you have rubbed with either a cut clove of garlic or a shallot, mix with the roughly broken lettuce a good sprinkle of chervil tufts (not chopped) half a dozen leaves of tarragon, a dozen small leaves of rocket, three of basil, roughly broken, and about twenty spears of chives, chopped.

Egg Salad

Line some individual salad plates with tender leaves of lettuce heart. Pour over them mayonnaise and arrange slices of hard-boiled egg on this, half an egg per person. Sprinkle oil and wine vinegar on this and top with a sprinkle of mixed chopped parsley, tarragon and chervil. Olives, capers or chopped truffles all go well with egg and lettuce.

Herring Salad

Cook four salt herrings in a pint of water after they have been soaked. Cut these, six cold potatoes, two eating apples, four gherkins or two dill pickles, a tablespoonful of capers, a dozen olives, into strips. Chop a tablespoonful of parsley, one of young onion, one of chives, and one of chervil together, and mix with fish and potatoes, etc. Season plentifully with oil and vinegar and pile into a bowl adding at the last moment one cut-up beetroot.

Italian Salad

is for serving in early summer when new vegetables are tender and plentiful. Use young carrots, onions, turnips, peas, French beans, asparagus. Prepare and cook as for Julienne and put into a bowl with oil and vinegar, capers, salt and a teaspoonful of sugar. Leave for an hour then drain off the surplus water and substitute mayonnaise with a topping of chopped chervil and tarragon.

Russian Salad

is exactly similar ingredients, cut in small dice. Mix with mayonnaise as in the previous recipe.

Japanese Salad

Cook some small waxy potatoes in salted water in their jackets. While still hot cut them in slices into oil and wine vinegar in a bowl where you have sprinkled some chopped chervil and parsley. Add half as many mussels as potatoes (to cook and open mussels see recipe for marinated mussels), add salt, pepper, chopped tarragon, two or three leaves of basil, some vine tips and sliced raw button mushrooms. Mix well.

Leeks with Pimentos

Cut a pound of young leeks into half-inch slices and cook gently in olive oil. Add two pimentos cut in small pieces, a sherry glass of white wine, half a dozen coriander seeds, a bay leaf, a spoonful of grated lemon rind and a teaspoonful of chopped parsley with the juice of half a lemon, Leave the leeks and pimentos to soak in it and serve cold.

Macedoine Provçenal

One pound small new potatoes, one pound small tomatoes quartered, three medium onions, chopped. Chop also a clove of garlic, some chives, fennel and tarragon, with two leaves of lemon balm and two of basil. Add a tablespoonful of capers, twelve black olives, oil, vinegar and grated lemon rind, all of which are pounded together for a sauce and added to the chopped vegetables.

Marrows

Take the very small kind of vegetable marrow known as courgettes, not more than eight inches long and three inches fat. Cut them into quarters and cook them in a Court Bouillon (see bouillabaise) in which is included half a teaspoonful of saffron and one part of oil to three parts water. Let them cool in this and dress with oil and vinegar sprinkled with chopped chervil.

Mushrooms

Small button mushrooms make a delightful salad or hors d'œuvre dropped into boiling salted water with a tablespoonful of lemon juice (to preserve the colour) for five minutes, then soaked in boiling marinade (made as usual) and left in it for 24 hours.

Nasturtium

Either the flowers or leaves or both make a delightful and pungent addition to a green salad if used with discretion. The large leaves may also have a spoonful of any kind of finely minced meat or vegetable stuffing put on them, be rolled up and tied with cotton and simmered for five minutes in a Court Bouillon. Serve cold with a mayonnaise into which two tablespoonfuls of whipped cream have been mingled.

I have a recipe for **Ostrich Egg Salad,** but unless you live in South Africa or a Zoo, it might be rather difficult to come by the essential ingredient. If you can get one, cook it for twenty minutes, if not, be content with a goose egg and cook it for ten. Put in cold water, shell and cut in halves long ways. Remove the yolk, mangle it up a little with some mayonnaise and cream cheese, put back piled up in the whites and decorate the mounds with a curled anchovy at each end, a scatter of chervil along the middle, and a radish fuchsia at the centre point.

Potato Salad

Choose the yellow Dutch kind if possible, they do not disintegrate, and boil them gently in their skins which improves the flavour enormously. Cut them up, *while hot*, into a mixture of oil and vinegar into which you have introduced a suspicion of garlic, a tablespoonful of parsley, a teaspoonful of chervil and half a teaspoonful of tarragon, all chopped. Turn about gently in the mixture and do not break the slices of potato. When well mixed add shreds of anchovy and some sliced marinated mushrooms (see earlier recipe).

Prussian Salad

is very similar to the foregoing, except that it contains two eating apples sliced, chopped chives and sliced salt herring instead of anchovy. Just as it is ready to serve add a medium sized beetroot cut in small dice. If beetroot is mingled earlier it will suffuse the whole mixture and look very messy.

Salade d'Endive

Shred the skin of two oranges in long fine strips and boil these for five minutes to blanch away the bitterness as one does with cabbages. Drain and dry the strips and cut up the flesh, removing the membranes. Take two well-blanched curled endives and wash, then dry the blanched hearts pulling them to pieces in a bowl. Sprinkle with salt and a little sugar then with chopped tarragon and the orange flesh. Pour over them Sauce Chantilly, which is mayonnaise with the addition of whipped cream, and strew carelessly all over the top of this the orange strips.

Purslane Salad

is prepared exactly like lettuce or endive, then mixed with pimpernel, tarragon and chervil, all chopped.

Salade Suédoise

is watercress dressed with oil and lemon juice then mixed with slices of sweet apple and sprinkled with chopped fennel and marjoram.

Tomatoes, as a Vegetable

Hollow them, mix the contents with boiled rice, olive oil, chopped garlic and chopped mint with a half teaspoonful of paprika and plenty of pepper and salt. Pile this back in the tomatoes, put on their lids again, cook, and serve with roast lamb.

Another recipe begins in the same way, but stuffs the cavities with fried onion, bread crumbs, anchovies, capers, parsley, all chopped together, and when the lids are replaced more crumbs mixed with olive oil are sprinkled over before baking about half an hour.

Yet another recipe calls for all the above plus a medium can of tuna fish, half teaspoonful of basil and the same of marjoram, chopped. It is baked in the same way.

Vine Leaves, Stuffed (Armenian)

Take plenty of young tender vine leaves. Cook a pound of finely chopped onions in four tablespoonfuls of olive oil, add a quarter-pound of uncooked rice, cover after it has browned in the oil and cook until rice is tender, about half an hour. Add 2 tablespoonfuls chopped parsley, 2 tablespoonfuls chopped raisins, 2 tablespoonfuls chopped pine nuts or almonds, ½ cup of tomato paste, 1 teaspoonful allspice, ½ teaspoonful marjoram, salt and pepper to taste, and cook all together about five minutes, stirring all the time. Have ready a baking dish with a layer of sliced onions and a layer of vine leaves. On other vine leaves lay small heaps of the mixture, one spoonful on each, and roll up, turning over the ends like small parcels, then packing side by side on the foundation of other leaves, until all the stuffing is used up. Each person usually eats at least six. Add a small cupful of water to the pan, cover with a lid and bake gently for an hour. You can either eat them hot from the dish or allow to cool in their own juice and serve cold, speared with a cocktail stick as an appetizer.

Vine Salad

In late June when the growth is very tender pick a good handful of young tips and tendrils. They will be cut off anyway. Pop them into cold water under a running tap for ten minutes, then into a large pan of boiling salted water for five minutes. Drain and dress with oil, walnut if possible, olive if not, wine vinegar, a dozen tender young black currant leaves from the tips of young shoots, chopped chervil, tarragon and parsley, and after turning and mixing well, serve very cold.

Another version of the stuffed vine leaves calls for a filling of minced meat, boiled rice, chopped parsley and thyme, with pepper and salt, fried onion, and a raw egg to bind it. Then one proceeds as with the herb-stuffed ones, rolling into parcels, tying with cotton, and stewing in stock flavoured with tomato paste.

INDEX